Winter

By Terri DeGezelle

Consultant:
Joseph M. Moran, Ph.D.
Meteorologist
Education Program
American Meteorological Society

Bridgestone Books
an imprint of Capstone Press
Mankato, Minnesota

Bridgestone Books are published by Capstone Press
151 Good Counsel Drive, P.O. Box 669, Mankato, Minnesota 56002
http://www.capstone-press.com

Library of Congress Cataloging-in-Publication Data
DeGezelle, Terri, 1955–
    Winter / by Terri DeGezelle.
    p. cm.—(Seasons)
    Includes bibliographical references and index.
    Contents: Winter—Winter temperatures—Water in winter—Trees in winter—Animals in winter—People in winter—What causes winter?—Why do seasons change?—Seasons in other places—Hands on : earth's tilt in winter.
    ISBN 0-7368-1412-4 (hardcover)
    1. Winter—Juvenile literature. [1. Winter.] I. Title.
QB637.8 .D44 2003
509.2—dc21   2001008759

Summary: Explains why seasons change and describes the ways trees, animals, and people react to winter.

Editorial Credits
Christopher Harbo, editor; Karen Risch, product planning editor; Linda Clavel, designer and illustrator; Anne McMullen, illustrator; Alta Schaffer, photo researcher

Photo Credits
Corbis, cover (bottom left)
Dave G. Houser/Houserstock, 4
International Stock/Caroline Wood, 14
Kent & Donna Dannen, 6, 12
Photri-Microstock/Skjold, cover (main photo)
Richard Hamilton Smith, 8
Timothy C. Harbo, 21
Unicorn Stock Photos/Martha McBride, cover (top left), 10; Jeff Greenberg, 20

Artistic Effects
Corbis; Unicorn Stock Photos/Martha McBride

1 2 3 4 5 6 07 06 05 04 03 02

Table of Contents

Fun Fact

The first day of winter is called the winter solstice.

4

Winter

Winter is the season between autumn and spring. In the Northern Hemisphere, the first day of winter is December 21 or 22. Winter lasts for three months. Winter is the coldest season of the year.

hemisphere
one half of Earth

Fun Fact

North America's coldest recorded temperature happened in Snag, Yukon, Canada. The temperature was minus 81 degrees Fahrenheit (minus 63 degrees Celsius) on February 3, 1947.

Winter Temperatures

Outdoor temperatures in winter can be very cold. Cold winds blow and make the air feel even colder. People stay in their houses. Some animals huddle together to stay warm.

Fun Fact

Silver Lake, Colorado, holds the record for the most snowfall in 24 hours. More than 6 feet (1.8 meters) of snow fell on April 14 and 15, 1921.

Water in Winter

Many lakes and ponds freeze in winter. Blizzards sometimes happen during winter. Heavy snows fall in the mountains. Rain falls in the southern part of the Northern Hemisphere.

blizzard
a heavy snowstorm with strong winds

Trees in Winter

Most trees do not have leaves during winter. Only pine, spruce, and other evergreen trees are green in winter. The soil freezes in many parts of the Northern Hemisphere. Trees cannot get water from the soil until spring.

Animals in Winter

Many animals have trouble finding food in winter. Squirrels gather and store food for the cold months. Birds look for seeds in bird feeders. Some animals hibernate in winter. Bears sleep in dens.

 hibernate
to spend winter in a deep sleep

People in Winter

People dress warmly in winter. They wear winter coats, hats, mittens, and snow boots to keep warm. Children can go sledding and skiing. They can build a snowman. Schools close during blizzards.

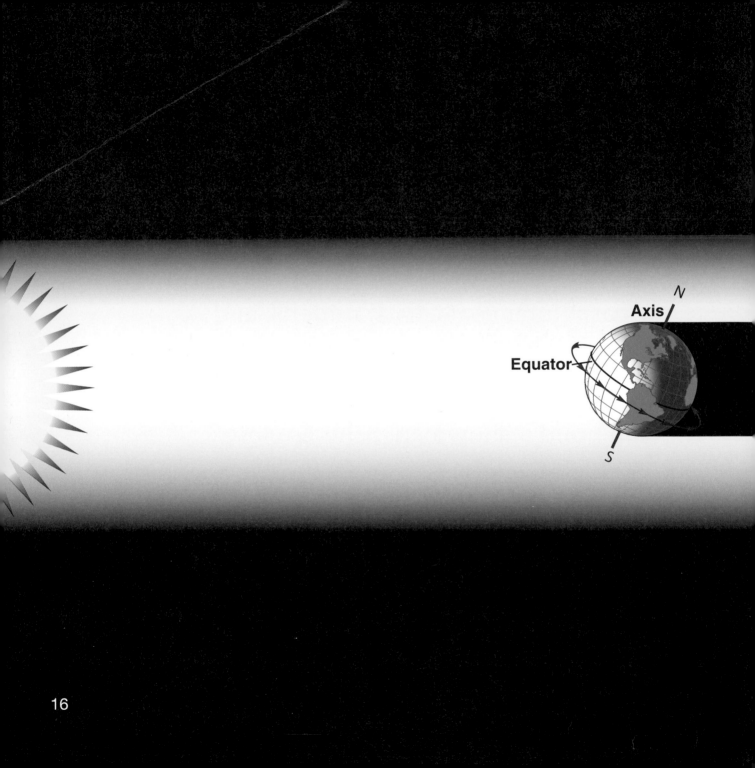

What Causes Winter?

Earth's tilt causes winter. Earth spins like a top as it moves around the Sun. Earth spins on an axis. The axis is tilted. Winter begins when Earth's axis points away from the Sun. On the first day of winter, the Sun's rays center on places south of the equator.

axis

an imaginary line that runs through the middle of Earth from the North Pole to the South Pole

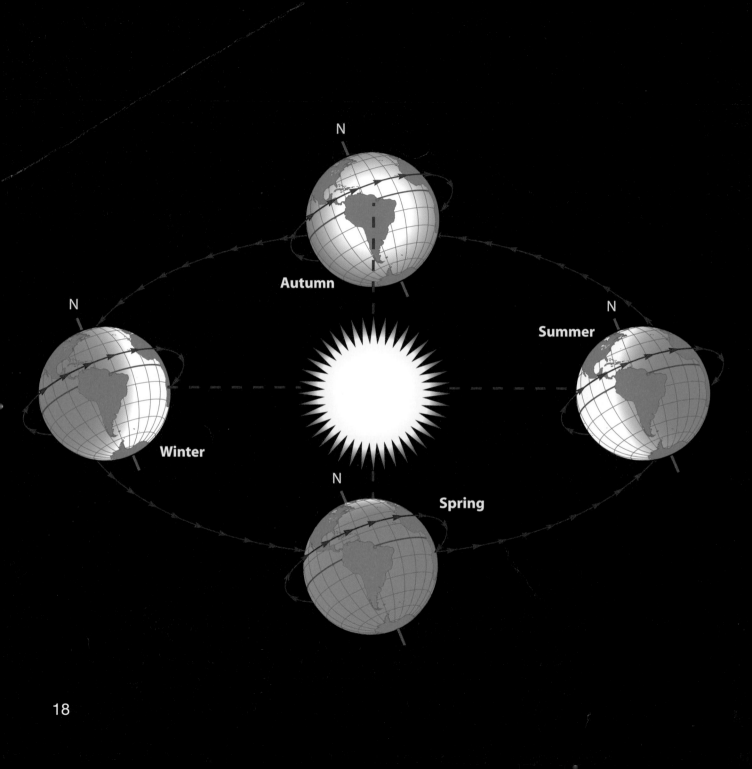

Autumn

Summer

Winter

Spring

Why Do Seasons Change?

Earth makes one trip around the Sun each year. Earth's movement and tilt cause seasons to change. The Northern Hemisphere leans away from the Sun in winter. The Sun is low in the sky. Daylight is shortest in winter.

When the Northern Hemisphere has winter, the Southern Hemisphere has summer. People celebrate New Year's Eve dressed for cold weather in the Northern Hemisphere.

In the Southern Hemisphere, many people spend New Year's Day at the beach. They wear shorts and T-shirts.

Hands On: Earth's Tilt in Winter

Earth's tilt causes the seasons. During winter, the North Pole points away from the Sun. Less sunlight hits the Northern Hemisphere. You can see how Earth's tilt creates winter.

What You Need

Globe
Table
Flashlight

What You Do

1. Place the globe on the table.
2. Tilt the globe slightly away from you.
3. Take five steps back from the globe.
4. Shine the flashlight at the globe. Hold the flashlight so that the brightest spot shines on the Tropic of Capricorn in the Southern Hemisphere. The Tropic of Capricorn is an imaginary line about halfway between the equator and the South Pole.

The globe's tilt causes most of the flashlight's beam to shine on the Southern Hemisphere. Sunlight shines on Earth during winter in the same way. Look at the North Pole. It receives almost no sunlight all day or all night during winter.

Words to Know

axis (AK-siss)—an imaginary line that runs through the middle of Earth from the North Pole to the South Pole
blizzard (BLIZ-urd)—a heavy snowstorm with strong winds
equator (i-KWAY-tur)—an imaginary line halfway between the North Pole and the South Pole
hemisphere (HEM-uhss-fihr)—one half of Earth; the Northern Hemisphere is north of the equator.
hibernate (HYE-bur-nate)—to spend winter in a deep sleep
season (SEE-zuhn)—one of four parts of the year; winter, spring, summer, and autumn are seasons.
tilt (TILT)—an angle to the left or right of center

Read More

Burke, Jennifer S. *Cold Days.* Weather Report. New York: Children's Press, 2000.

Burton, Jane, and Kim Taylor. *The Nature and Science of Winter.* Exploring the Science of Nature. Milwaukee: Gareth Stevens, 1999.

Stille, Darlene R. *Winter.* Simply Science. Minneapolis: Compass Point Books, 2001.

Internet Sites

FEMA For Kids: Winter Storms
http://www.fema.gov/kids/wntstrm.htm
**NOVA Online: Japan's Secret Garden—Secrets of
    Hibernation**
http://www.pbs.org/wgbh/nova/satoyama/
    hibernation.html
Science U—Seasons Reasons
http://www.scienceu.com/observatory/articles/
    seasons/seasons.html

Index